The Incredible Bulk,The Story of the Federal Debt.

SORCES

I www.mrconservative.com Obama made no clear statement on jail time for not enrolling in Obama Care,Obama says that there is $1,000.00 hidden tax on American families because people don't have health
insurance

II Against Crony Capitalism.org 4th amendment The right of the people to be secure in their persons,houses,papers,and effects,against unreasonable searches and seizures,shall not be violated and warrants shall issue,but upon probable cause,supported by Oath or affirmation and particularly describing the place to be searched,and the persons or things to be seized.

III Alliance Defending Freedom A 10 year old Katie Ayers tried handing out invitations to her churches Christmas party which was denied,she won the case and appeals.

IV Stop Amnesty With 20,000,000 Americans still out of work Congress should not reward 11,000,000 illeagal alians with lifetime work permits.

V Capitalism Institute The Suprem Court ruled that the States are not merely polictical subdivisions of the federal goverrnment to carry out what the federal government doles out;they are sovereign entities. Congress can pass laws,but it cannot compel the states to utilize either their treasury or personnel to implement them.

VI Bankrupting America 25% strongly approve of Obama Care 43% strongly disapprove 66% agree the failure of Obama Care"prove that the federal government shouldn't rush into any more big expensive projects"This survey was conducted by the Tarrance group via land line and cell phone from December 1-5 2013,among 803 registered voters throughout the county.It has a margin of error +/- 3.5 percent.

VII The New Republic of Texas Promise Obama said Obama Care would lower premiums by $2,500 Reality Will increase health care cost by $7,540 for a family of four.

V www.capitalisminstitute.org Rand Paul is taking the NSA to the Suprem Court.

VIII The New Republic of Texas There is no worse tyranny than to force a man to pay for what he does not want merely because you think it would be good for him. Robert Heinlein.

IX The Foundry Common Core Fifth grade teachers,for example have been told to follow a new,scripted 500 page curriculum pretty much to the letter,Cost 46 states that singed on $40,000,000,000 over the next 7 years.

X Washington Examiner Lawmakers have stood idly by,for example,as courts redefined the handling of captured enemy combatants,giving them more rights than they are entitled to under the Geneva Conventions an putting US forces at a disadvantage in fighting terrorists.

V Capitalism Institute Article five of the US Constitution gives us the power to amend it.One of the options it details is a convention of states ,where an amendment is proposed by two-thirds of the states (a minimum 34)and,to be ratified must receive the approval of three-fourths of the states(a minimum of 38)Congress has ratified all amendments so far and with their 9% approval rating the states are taking the charge to fight tyranny.

XI Personal Liberty Digest 97% of americans want their old health care system back.

XII After 2 years of Obama january 2009-2011 avg.retail price/gallen gas US $1.83 $3.95 change 115.8% sorce 1

Crude oil,European Brent(barrel)$43.48 $99.02 change 127.7% sorce 2

Crude Oil,West TX International barrel $38.79 $91.38 change 135.9% sorce 2

Gold:London(per troy onch)$857.25 $1504.50 change 90.5% sorce 2Soybeans,No 1 yellow Il $9.66 $13.75 change 42.3% sorce 2Corn No2 yellow Central Il $3.56 $6.33 change 78.1% sorce 2Surgar cane raw World lb Fol $13.37 $35.39 change 164.7% sorce2Unemployment rate non farm 7.6% 9.4% change 23.7% sorce 3Unemployment rate black 12.6% 15.8% change 25.4% sorce 3Number of federal employees 2,799,000 2,840,000 change 2.2% sorce 3Number of unemployed 11,616,000 14,485,000 change 24.7% sorce 3Real median household income $50,112 $49,777 change 0.7% sorce4Number of unemployment benifit recipients 7,526,58 9,193,838 change 22.2% sorce 6Number of long term unemployed 2,600,000 6,400,000 change 146.3% sorce 3Poverty rate individuals 13.2% 14.3% change 8.3% sorce 4People in poverty in US 39,800,00 43,600,00 change 9.5% sorce 4US rank in economic freedom world rankings 5 9 n/a 10Present situation index 29.9 23.5 change -21.4% sorce 11Failed banks 140 164 change 17.1% sorce 12US dollar verses Japanese yen exchange rate 89.76 82.03 change -8.6% sorce 2US money supply M1 in billions 12,575.1 1,865..7 change 18.4% sorce 2US money supply M2 in billions 8,310.9 8,852.3 change 6.5% sorce 13

National debt in trillions $10.627 $14.052 change 32.2% sorce 14

Just take this last item :In the last two years we have accumulated national debt at a rate more than 27 times as fast as during the rest of our entire nations history.Over 27 times as fast.Metaphorically speaking ,If you are driving in the right lane doing 65 mph and a car rockets past you in the left lane 27 times faster it would be doing 7,555 mph.What would the speeding ticket be like for this one? sorces1 US Energy Information Administration.2 Wall Street Journal.3 Bureau of Labor Statistics.4 Census Bureau.5 USDA.6 US Dept of labor.7 FHFA.8 Stand & Poors Case Shiller.9 Reality Trac;10 Heritage Foundation and WSJ:11The Conference Board;12 FDIC,13 Federal Reserve.14 US Treasury.XII   WAGESSalary of retired US Presidents $450,000Salary of House Senate members $174,000Salary of Speaker of the House $223,500Salary of Majority/Minority Leaders $194,400Average salary of a soldier deployed in afghanistan $38,000

Average income for seniors on Social Security $12,000$7.544 billion annual contribution to UN.
WAR X We are at war with terrorists and there is no way we can win if we give terrorists more rights than are granted by the Geneva Convention.Our military must be given the freedom to attack any enemy target of military sinifigance Our soldiers need to know that they have our full support Anyone that would put our troops in harms way without making a commitment to win the war is guilty of mass-murder in the eyes God!Our weapons and equipment must be maintained in good working order and our soldiers need regular training.When we go to war we need to hit the enemy with everything we have and don't let up until they surrender.The only way we can avoid a war is to be so strong that no enemy would dare attack.To take from our vetrans to give to illegal aliens is treason!

Illegal Aliens IV We need to stop amnesty so we don't appear weak to the world community and weaken our economy.Illeagal aliens by definition don't respect our laws.Amnesty also gives enemys a oportunity to dump their criminals on us.No one that enters this nation illegaly should not be allowed to vote.Deporting them quickly can reduce the amont of money we spend houseing them

Foreing AidWe need to cut foreing aid.except to help Israrel.but we can't make them dependant on us.If we give money to terrorist nations to help their citizens they will hold them hostage until they enslave the world.If a nation can't run their economy on their own productivity they will be a burden on the rest of the world.There is nothing wrong in teaching how to improve their economy.We need a healthy balance between cooperation and compettion.One thing is true on a group or individual level.If hard work dosen't get results there is no reason to work and we will be equaly misrable.We needto turn up the preasure on those who favor giving money to hostil nations. Securety IV With 11,000,000 illegal aleians in our nation there is a great risk of terrorist coming to carry out attacts.With many of them on public assistance they can drain our economy.For securety we need a work force that is loyal to our constitution. Our right to bear arms can help our secureity if we recieve proper training.VII How can we be secure if we can't trust our elected officals to be honest.X We are at war with terrorist and we can't win this war if they have more rights than granted by the Geneva Convention,especially they don't abide by our rules.

InventionsII The 4th amendment gives us the right to withhold information on our ideas until the proper time,so we are secure enough to put in the,effort,money,and risk neceary to develope the idea to it's logical conclusion.IX In order to encorage innovation to improve our standard of living we need to teach the next generation to think.V A convention of states may be a way to pass a constitutional amendment to reward creativity.A first to invent system is cheaper and faster than first to file.For first to invent you need a approved inventors log book and fill it out according to rules.Under first to file you would need a patent attorney and for improvements you would file a motion that is as expensive as a patent application.For first to invent you log your improvements in your log book.Not all creative people have deep pockets.For further details contact the Inventors Assistance League.Toll free (877)433-2246 phone (818)246-6546 email help@inventions.org web www.inventions.org.address 1053 Colorado Blvd,

TaxVII There is no worse tyranny than to force a man to pay for what he does not want merely because it would be good for him.Robert Heinlein This this why we need to have a way of knowing how our tax money is being spent Artists should be able to solicate funds from people that believe in their work,but they shouldn't get government funding enableing the government to use propaganda take away our freedoms.In my opinion the fair tax is the best substitute for our current system.It is a tax on goods and services offered to the public.A flat tax is better than what we have now.(a percentage everyone pays,no exemptions.)We need a simple tax code everyone can understand so that the government can't use confusion to get away with favoring one group over another.A simple tax code will be cheaper to enforce because it is easyer to determine how much is owed.Under the fair tax there would be fewer enities paying taxes so it would to be easyer to catch cheats.The fair tax would make it harder to avoid taxes with secerect bank accounts.

United NationsXII We are giving $7.544 billion to the United Nations every year not counting peace keeping forces and emergency humanitarian aid.I don't have the figures for what the peace keeping and humanitarian aid cost,but it is obvious that it would cost something to send equipment and fuel to wherever the mission is.The soldiers have to be paid and fed.They are underpaid for the work they do.The aid we give to these dictatorships frees up resorces for their agenda.It is a safe bet that they are diverting the humanitarian aid for other purposes.We must come against anything that looks like a world tax that can endanger our sovernty.The European Union can endanger national sovernty for the above mentioned reasons.

Government BenfitsThe government is obligated to provide for the common defense and to protect our freedoms.If the church would take responsiblity seriously (everyone that claims to be christian.)the government wouldn't need to get involved.Every able bodied person should be requierd to do something to recieve benfits.Voluntere work,picking up trash along highways cleaning cemetaryes,,assisting those who can't do daily chores that need to be done,visiting the sick and/or infirm.I would recommend training on how to spot and report abuse.With all the people on welfare it will take time to train them to do things indepenant of the welfare system,but it will be a good investment,and help them feel good about themselves.Recieving assistance is nothing to be ashamed of,but you should at least have a desire to contribute.How many veterins would like to talk to school children?We need to instill a respect for our military in the next generation.

Health CareI Obama Care is a hidden tax because of the fines and manditory coverage most people don't need.A failed web-site is another drain on our economy.Comparing it to car insurance isn't fair because one legal way to avoid car insurance is don't own a car.II Obama Care violates the 4th amendment by seizing our money without due process,and alll the private information that it collects.There is evidence of serious security problems.With Obama making changes at a whim without congress challening him is a serious threat to our freedoms.IV 11,000,000 illeaguel aliens recieveing free health care is dumb.They should be deported without benifits.If granted leaguel status they could sponser friends and family at government exspense.Securing our borders to prevent the problem would be a good idea.V this would seem to indicate that the states could refuse to accept illeaguel aliens solving a problem the federal government won't deal with.VI This shows that most americans don't want our government taking on expensive projects that are none of their business.XI 97% of americans want their old health care system back.   Warrenty We need to get a warrenty on all goods and services purchased by the government so that the manufactuers do it right the first time or make it right at their exspense.No more cost overruns.If they can't make a reasonable profit with their origional bid,they should make a more realistic bid.We need to get all of our goods and services from at least two sorces ,with each company recieveing a minimum percentage of contracts and companyies competing to increase their share.We need to keep a eye on the government so they don't

play a shell game to favor one company over another at our expenes.Our represenativs must not be allowed to benifit from any company that the government does business with.We need to keep records of how well companies honor their warrenties.If a private citizen can get a warrenty the government should be able to do the same.
Private PropertyThe 4th amendment states the right of the people to be secure in their persons,houses papers(This inclueds electronic information to),and effects(private property)against unreasonable search and seizuers.should not be violated and no warrent shall issue,but upon probable cause,supported by oath or affirmation and particularly describing the place to be searched,and the persons or things to be seized.This amendment can encourage economic productivity because people know that the fruit of their labor can't be arbitarly seized.This amendment limits search and seizers so that warrents can't be used to harrass political dissidents.The oath affirmation helps the judge to make his/her decision on accurate information.People can work better if they don't have to worry about unreasonable arrest.IV People would have a easyer time finding work if everyone in this country were here leaugly.And a work force deticated to america could make this nation strong.V The supprem court ruled that states are not merely political subdivisons of the federal government to carryout what the federal government doles out.They are sovereign

enities.Congress can pass laws,but it can't commpell states to utilize treasury or personnel to implement those federal laws.This gives the states a tool to limit the growth of the federal government in order to protect the rights of the people.V The NSA spying can place private ownership at risk by targeting those who disagree with the government.VIII This can refer to Obama Care,forced union dues,or the theory of evolution.(If you want to believe it that is your business,but don't shove it down our throate.XI 97% of americans want their old health care system back again,Obama Care is not working!XII The increase in price of gas,food,cost of living,and decrease in income means less productivity,and the increase in the money supply contributes to inflation which is a hidden tax.The national debt means less revenue for economic recovery.With the national debt increasing at 27 times as fast as the rest of our history in the last two years you can't convince me that there is no more spending cuts to be made.Our representatives should be paid for there time in office and then get a job in the private sector.

T Free market trade is vital for maintaining the economy of any civilization.Competition will encourage companies to provide high quality at low prices in order to increase their market share.Trade between nations can enable them to do what they are good at.We need to have guidelines in place to prevent currency manipulation so national leaders can benifit on the merit of the goods and services they offer that others are willing to pay for. People need to know that there is no limit on what they are allowed to earn in order to encourage them to do their best

The following information is from NASA's web-site

(NASA's Asteroid Initiative has two main parts: a mission to identify, robotically capture, and redirect a small asteroid into a stable lunar orbit; and a grand challenge to promote global collaboration in finding all asteroid threats to human populations and know what to do about them.)once captured the asteroid can be mined for profit solving two problems.With a potential of over $20,000,000,000,000 of material per asteroid it would be well worth the risk for what it could add to our economy.The abundance of gold,iron,platinum,and other resorces can be used to supply space colionies. We would be able to build space stations for research and tourism.Restruants would be a big draw once we get the money to build them.Hotels is a good idea to. I would start with a station with modeuals so it can be added to when more money is available.Each modeual would have a telescope and behind it there would be a lab for experiments for research.Get more than one the images from each could be put together for a sharper image of distance objects.Mabey we could rent to NASA.The public might be willing to log on to view the images for a fee. Radio-active waste could be sent to space for research for produceing artifical elements that are not radio-active.What ifb web could come up with nutronium(a substance mentioned on star-treck).This would solve the problem of storeing them on earth and make it harder for terrorist to steal them for dirty bombs.This would make it nessasary to drasticaly reduce the cost of putting a payload in orbit. High teperature super-conductors would make a magnetic bottles for containing plasma for propelent possible.Hydrogen can be heated by atomic power laysors and a group of laysors can be at the nozzel to use shock-waves to compress the plasma to initiate fussion.It can be timed to produce 1,000's of explodshions per second.A robot ship wont need life-support and can operate at G-forces not compatible with human life.High speed computers could control them for deep space minning.As we get ships that approch the speed of light we will have to take time dilation into consideration because time will slow down for the ship. Mabey some of our vetrens could get jobs as security in order to protect the space population.Combat experiance can help them deal with crime.We will need laws that can be enforced for the society to function.A space currancy independant of national money supply will help.We will also need service workers to Water will be nessasary for this socity and I belive that the best place to get it would be from commets and water moons in our solar system.We will need to have water treatment systems simmular to that used aboard the space-station.Water sports would be a big draw.Your imagination is the limit. The moon would be a good place to test new propulsion systems because if something goes wrong it wont endanger populations on earth.The cold side of the moon would help test super-conducting materials before high-temperature super-conductors are invented because refrideration wouldent be needed.We would learn how much fuel is needed for the desired thrust.Super light-weight materials could make larger and faster ships possible. This will make space funerals possible.Options would be earth-orbit,flight into the sun,other planets,crash landing on the moon,and leaving the solar system.Different theams would be possible.

In recent years, the objectives of our nation's space program have grown increasingly sophisticated and ambitious. Future missions will focus on exploration at greater distances from Earth and extended stays in space. To ensure that these goals are achieved, NASA's astronauts must be able to perform at peak productivity under even the most daunting conditions. The Human Research Program is dedicated to discovering the best methods and technologies to support safe, productive human space travel. From the challenges of providing appetizing food and optimal nutrition to managing the environmental risks posed by radiation and lunar dust, HRP scientists and engineers work to predict, assess, and solve the problems that humans encounter in space. Planned future missions will dramatically increase the scope of the challenges and demands that face NASA's astronauts. The HRP is working to improve astronauts' ability to collect data, solve problems, respond to emergencies, and remain healthy during and after extended space travel. Part of HRP's mission is to educate the public about the challenges of human space travel. As you navigate this site, you can learn more about the research and technology that supports and facilitates the work of the men and women who navigate the outer reaches of space.) This artical shows the importance of taking care of human health.One russhian cosmonaut spent one year in space and when he returned to earth he was to weak to stand up in earths gravity.We need artifical

gravity for long term space flight to keep musscels and bones strong.It has been estemated that 5 years in a zero gravity enviorment wrould make bones so weak that as slap on the back would shatter the spine.I wonder what 5 years in a 2 g enviorment would do. One way to ensure that our astronaunts produce safely and efficently is to record phycological reactions.See if color makes any differance.We need appetizing food that provides the needed nutrition,which will become easyer when the station gets bigger and the cost of getting equipment and high quality food in space is greatly reduced.Choice can help the moral of our astronauts. One solution for the radiation problem that should be studied is to make the skin of the station with a outer layer of depleated uranium,middel layer lead,inner layer aluminum.If research shows problems at lest we would have learned something.We need to study the different types of radiation fond in space.
(Orion Multi-Purpose Crew Vehicle This spacecraft will serve as the primary crew vehicle for missions beyond low Earth orbit. The Orion MPCV is capable of conducting regular in-space operations (rendezvous, docking, extravehicular activity) in conjunction with payloads delivered by the Space Launch System for missions beyond low Earth orbit. The spacecraft also has the capability to be a backup system for International Space Station cargo and crew delivery) This can help our economy by making space profitable.This vehicle can be use for

experiments that lead to new inventions that will provide jobs on earth.It can serve as a emergency escape vehicle,fire,leak,or anything else that endangers the crew. It can also serve as a system to deliver tools to a moon colony.If someone comes up with a idea for a new tool for use for work that they are doing,the desing can be beamed to the space-station for printing on a 3d printer.This can save time over delivery directly from provided that there is a ship in orbit at all times.It would also save cost over escaping earths gravity well every time we needed to make a delivery to the moon.

Paving the Way to Tomorrow (Imagine a spaceport of the future, where a variety of space vehicles are preparing for launch or departing Earth on missions to expand humanity's reach into space. At NASA's Kennedy Space Center in Florida, the Ground Systems Development and Operations Program, formerly known as the 21st Century Ground Systems Program, is propelling this vision forward, leading the center's transformation from a historically government-only launch complex to a spaceport bustling with activity involving government and commercial vehicles alike. The program's primary objective is to prepare the center to process and launch the next-generation vehicles and spacecraft designed to achieve NASA's goals for space exploration. To achieve this transformation, program personnel are developing the necessary ground systems while refurbishing and upgrading infrastructure and facilities to meet

tomorrow's demands. This modernization effort keeps flexibility in mind, in order to accommodate a multitude of government, commercial and other customers. Drawing on five decades of experience -- and excellence -- in processing and launch, the Ground Systems Development and Operations Program is paving the way to the spaceport's future.) A spaceport would be necessary to facilitate space commerence.In my opinion a privatley owned spaceport that accepts private and government customers would be best for our economy because free market forces would encourage high quality and low prices,and it can encourage competitive wages.A government monopoly offers no incentive to improve. A atom smasher on the dark side of the moon would help rescearch into the basic structure of mater.Since it would be located on the dark side of the moon it would be easier to keep the magnecs superconducting since the temmparature would be below -200Farunheight.If the reseharcers stayed away from the dark side of the moon when the atom smasher is running it can be on the surface since the moon would provide the neccsary sheilding from the radiation that would be produced.The information could be sent to rescearch teams on earth. If colonist on the other side of the moon could dig below the surface of the moon the mass of the moon could provide sheilding from radiation.The layers of rock can provide insulation from temmpature extereams.
The following information is from NOAA's web-

site.

Technology

Today's technologies allow us to explore the ocean in increasingly systematic, scientific, and noninvasive ways. With continuing technological advances, our ability to observe the ocean environment and its resident creatures is beginning to catch up with our imaginations, expanding our understanding and appreciation of this still largely unexplored realm.
This section of the Ocean Explorer website highlights the technologies that make today's explorations possible. These technologies include platforms such as vessels and submersibles, observing systems and sensors, communication technologies, and diving technologies that transport us across ocean waters and into the depths, allowing us to examine, record, and analyze the mysteries of the ocean.

Vessels
(Platforms: Vessels

From onboard equipment to collect weather and ocean information to divers, submersibles, and other observations deployed from a ship, vessels are the most critical tool for scientists when it comes to exploring the ocean.
Submersibles
Platforms: Submersibles)

Floating platforms can be used to send vessels to the ocean floor to collect data and plant sensors.it can also be used to map the ocean floor to help establish colonies of research personel.
 The underwater stations can be built on the surface in modual forms that can be added to when additional revenue is made addvailable.This can help these communities to grow. These structures would have tanks that could be flooded when it comes time to send them to the ocean floor.The one in the deepest part of the ocean floor would have to withstand pressures greater than 8tons per square inch.
 These underwater communities can use deep sea vessels to collect sampells,map the ocean floor,and record the different life forms.Pictures of the life in the ocean can be sent to the surface to provide real time information for floating zoos that can raise money by charging a fee to view them.
 This can help mining operations and drilling for oil and natterual gas.Mineral resorhces mayby discovered.Deep sea vessels can be used to bring these resorches safely to the surface.

Floating restaurants can serve tourist that come to see the sights and if the under water community can order the meals that appeal to them it can help promote moral.This can help with special need diets.

A emergancy medical station both in under water communities and on the surface can help save lives by giving promet treatment and asshment of condition before sending them to the hospital.Medical supplies and doctors can be onsite for health and safety issues.

Regular inspections are nessasary to keep everyone safe.This will mean that we will need inspectors that have been trained to spot safety hazzards.they will also need to know how to correct them and athority to see to it that corrective action is taken.

Sensors to record temperature and water currents can help weather fore casts.Under water earth quakes can trigger suenomies and the better we are of giving advance warnings the more lives we can save.

The recommendations in this book can help reduce spending,payoff the debt,and increase revenue without any tax hikes.

The following bible verses illustrait basic princepals that can be applied to our national debt.
(Mt 22:17-22
17 Tell us there fore,What think thou?Is it lawful to give tribute unto Caesar,or not?

18 But Jesus perceived their wickedness,and said,Why tempt ye me,ye hypocrites?
19 Shew me the tribute money.And they brought unto him a penny.
20 And he saith unto them,Whose is this image and superscription?
21They say unto him,Caesars;Then saith he unto them,Render there fore unto Caesar the things which are Caesars;and unto God the things that are Gods.
22 When they herd these words they marvelled,and left him,went their way.)

Jesus precieved their hyporcy because if he answeard yes he would be trouble with the jewish people because they hated paying taxes,if he said no he would be in trouble with the roman government.

According to this scripture we should be paying our fair share of taxes and the government is responsible for how they use the money.

Mark 6:8 And commanded them that they should take nothing for their journy,save a staff only,nor script,no bread,nor money in their purse.

The desciples were among friends that should be able to help them.Just like we should provide for our soilders when we send them on a mission. We should provide food and shelter them because they shouldn'have to take food with them or provide their shelter since they lay their lives on the line.

(I Timothy 6:10 For the love of money is the root of all evil,which while some coveted after,they have erred from the faith,and pierced themselves though with many sarrows.)

Anyone that would do anything for money without regard for the laws of God or man is guilty of this sin weather he has a penny to his name or not.

This sin can lead to great sorrow because it leads to bad decissions,like bad relationships where there is no trust.Without rules there is no security for anyone.

This why some people don't help the needy,and some welfare recipents develop a entiltalment mentality.

(Mark 12:42-44

42 And their came a certain poor widow,and she thew in two mites,which make a farthing.

43 And he called unto him his decipales,and saith unto them.Verily I say unto you,That this poor widow hath cast more in,than all they which hath cast into the treasury.

44 For all they did cast of their abundance,but she of her want did cast in all that she had,even all her living.)

If we would learn from this scripture we would do the best we can unto God and our national productivity would go up and we could pay off our debt faster,save on interest,and our children wouldn't be burdened with the debt freeing up more money for essential functions.

Mt. 25:14-30

14 For the kingdom of heaven is as a man traveling into a far country,who called his own servants,and delivered unto them his goods.
15 And unto one he gave five talents,to another two,and to another one,to every man according to his serveral ability,and straightway took his journey.
16 Then he that had recieved the five talents went and traded with the same,and made other five talents.
17 And likewise he that had recieved two,he also gained other two.
18 But he that had recieved one went and digged in the earth,and hid his lords money.
19 After a long time the lord of those servants cometh and reconeth with them.
20 And so he that had recieved five talents,saying Lord,thou deliverdst unto me five talents:behold I have gained beside them five talents more.
21 His lord said unto him,Well done,thou good and faithful servant:thou hast been faithful over a few things.I will make thee ruler over many things:enter thou into the joy of thy lord.
22 He also that had recieved two talents came and said,Lord,thou deliverdst unto me two talents;I have two other talents beside them.
23 His lord said unto him,Well done good and faithful servant;thou hast been faithful over a few things,I will make thee ruler over many things,enter thou into the joy of thy lord.

24 Then he which had recieved the one talent came and said,Lord,I know thee that thou art a hard man,reaping where thou hast not strawed:
25 And I was afraid,and went and hid thy talent in the earth:lo,there thou hast that is thine.
26 His lord answered and said unto him,Thou wicked and slothful servant,thou knewest that I reap where I sowed not ,and gather where I have not strawed:
27 Thou oughtest there to have put my money to the exchangers,and then at my coming I should have recieved my own with usury.
28 Take therefore the talent from him,and give it unto him which hath ten talents.
29 For unto everyone that hath shall be given,and he shall have abundance,but from him that hath not shall be taken away even that which he hath.
30 And cast ye the unprofitable servant into outer darkness:there shall be weeping and gnashing of teeth.)

 These scriptures describe a basic principal of giving resorces to those that can make effeciant use of them.You give people what they can handel and when they do their best they are faithful.When some one won't use what they have been given,cut your loses and give to the one that can do the best job.This not a excuse to ignore the poor,but you don't have to support the lazy.The unprofitable servants reaction is a response to a loss that could have been avoided if he was willing to use what he had.

(Revelation 18:9-1

9 And the kings of the earth,who have commited fornication and lived deliciously with her,shall bewail her,and lament for her,when they shall see the smoke of her burning.

10 Standing afar off for the fear of her torment,saying,Alas,alas that great city,Babylon,that mighty city;for in one hour is thy judgement come.

11 And the merchants of the earth shall weep and mourn over her;for no man buyeth their merchandise anymore.

12 The merchandise of gold,and silver,and preciuos stones,and of pearls,and fine linen,and purple,and silk,and scarlet,and all thyine wood,and of brass,and iron,and marble.

13 And cinnamon,and odors,and ointments,and frankincense,and oil,and fine flour,and wheat,and beasts,and sheep,and horses,and chariots,and slaves,and souls of men.

14 And the fruits that thy soul lusted after are departed from thee,and all things which were dainty and goodly are departed from thee,and thou shall find them no more at all.

15 The merchants of these things,which were made rich by her,shall stand afar off for fear of her torment,weeping and wailing.

16 And saying,Alas,alas,that great city,that was clothed in fine linen,and purple,and scarlet,and decked with gold,and precious stones,and pearls.

17 For in one hour so great riches is come to nought.And every shipmaster,and all the company in ships and sailors,and as many as trade by sea,stood afar off.
18 And cried when they saw the smoke of her burning,and saying.What city is like unto this great city.
19 And they cast dust om their heads,and cried,weeping and wailing,saying.Alas,alas that great city,wherein were made rich all that ships in the sea by reason of her costliness,for in one hour is she made desolate.)

There is coming a time when the judgement of God will fall on this earth because the human race has rejected Gods ways.(Fourtuntly the church won't be here to experiance the wrath of God.)The kings of the earth are heads nations.The anti-christ will lead this one world government and will demand to be worshiped as God.

This scripture also shows the suffering produced by the love of money,slaves and souls of men.Their is evidence that cults will be trading human souls like commodities.

The weeping and wailing is proof of their extrem lust for money because what they looked to as their sorce is permantely gone.

The stage is being set with the entilealment mentality,people want security with little or no effort so they give up their freedom to a powerful central government and when the broken promises becomes obvious the government is powerful enough to maintain control though terror.

When the government controls the media it is easy to blame those that disagree with the government for the problems that plagge society.The solution would be for people to learn to do their own thinking and research the facts on their own.

We need to be able to limit the amount of information we give the government so that they can't use it to enslave us.If we repeal the income tax our income would be none of ther governments business.

The concentration of power will accelerate the deteriation of society by magnifying mans fallen nature.Man baseicaly has a selfish nature and we need learn how to care about others.

If mans basic nature was to put others first we would need few external laws because relationships would guide us to do what is nesasary for a prosperous economy.(Matthew 7:12)

Ezek 45:10 Ye shall have a just balance,and a just ephah,and a just bath.

This means that we need to be honest in our financial tranactons,a days pay for a days work.Making sure that the price for gods and/or services is clearly understood,and deliver exactly what is promised in quanity and quality.

This principal would help nations to get along with each other,and if the government would practice this principal we would getting our moneys worth from the taxes we pay.

A flat tax or fair tax mentioned earlyr in this book would also fit because they simple tax structures anyone can understand.

Inflation is a deceptive tax because it takes from us by eroding the value of our money.(In germany it reached 10% a hour.)This encourages borrowing for consumption and discourages saving,which means less capital for economic expansion.

(Matthew 20:20-28

20 Then came to him the mother of Zebedee's children with her sons,worshiping him,and desiring a certain thing of him.

21 And he said unto her,What wilt thou?She saith unto him,Grant that these my two sons may sit,the one on thy right hand,and the other on thy left in thy kingdom.

22 But Jesus answered and said and said,Ye know not what ye ask.Are ye able to drink of the cup that I shall drink of,and to be baptized with the baptism that I am baptized with?They say unto him,We are able.

23 And he saith unto them,Ye shall drink indeed of my cup,and be baptized with the baptism that I am baptized with:but to sit on my right hand,and on my left is not mine to give,but it shall be given to them for whom it is prepared of my father.

24 And when the ten heard it,they were moved with indignation against the two brethren.
25 But Jesus called them unto him,and said,Ye know that the princes of the gentiles exercise dominion over them,and they that are great exercise authority upon them.
26 But it shall not be so among you:but whosoever will be great among,let him be your minister.
27 And whosoever will be chief among you,let him be your servant:
28 Even the son of man came not to be ministered unto,but to minister,and to give his life a ransom for many.)

These scriptures portray the importance asinging athority to those that wil do the best job.The two desciples were trying to exalt themselves to high positions without realizing what is involved.

This can happen with politons that seek puplic office for their own benifit.This country will benifit when those that are in office realize that they are servants that work to make life better for all of us.

When Jesus said that the gentiles exercise dominion over them,and they that are great exercise authority upon them,he was pointing out the fact that it was about control,which will eventualy bring any society down.

Owners of businesses have to learn to be servants of all because customers make pay day possible.This principle will help employes because when they seek to serve that will cause everyone to work together for a common cause.There is power in unity.(Genesis 11:1-8)

Verses 22-23 tells of the importance of knowing the price of greatness be willing to pay the price.Fourtunaly God gives us the tools that we need.Verse 24 warns of the division caused by pride.

These scriptures also shows the importance of a chain of command that everyone respects in order to get a job done.

Jesus set the example by,healing the sick,rashing the dead,and the ultimate example when he suffered the most humelating and cruel death known to man to pay the penalty for our sins.

If anyone wants to become a part of Gods kingdom just pray this prayer,Lord Jesus I believe that you came from heaven to be born of a virgin,led a sinless life,went to the cross to pay the penalty for our sin in full,and obey you out of gratitude for your great sacrifice amen,If you prayed this prayer believing it in your heart you have just started your new life in Jesus.

www.ingramcontent.com/pod-product-compliance
Lightning Source LLC
Chambersburg PA
CBHW070727180526
45167CB00004B/1658